ANIMAL CHATTER

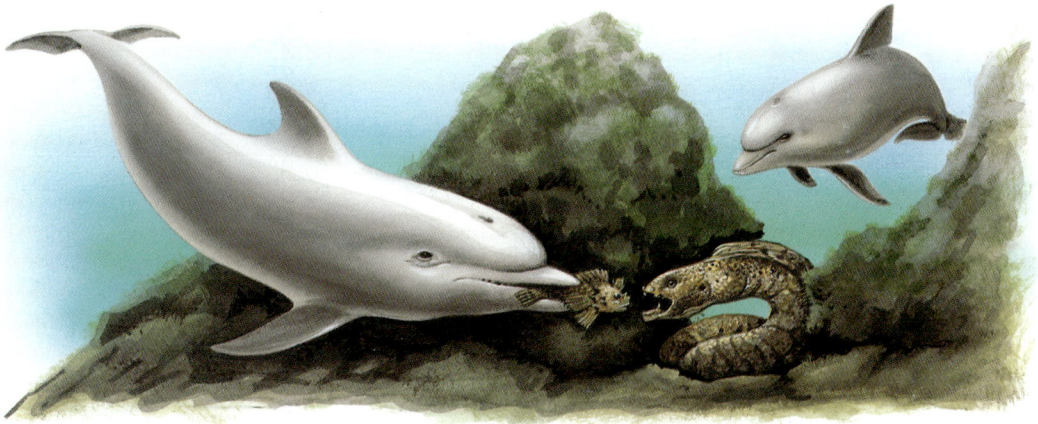

Kenna Bourke

OXFORD
UNIVERSITY PRESS

OXFORD
UNIVERSITY PRESS

Great Clarendon Street, Oxford OX2 6DP

Oxford University Press is a department of the University of Oxford.
It furthers the University's objective of excellence in research, scholarship,
and education by publishing worldwide in

Oxford New York

Auckland Bangkok Buenos Aires Cape Town Chennai
Dar es Salaam Delhi Hong Kong Istanbul Karachi Kolkata
Kuala Lumpur Madrid Melbourne Mexico City Mumbai
Nairobi São Paulo Shanghai Taipei Tokyo Toronto

Oxford is a registered trade mark of Oxford University Press
in the UK and in certain other countries

Published in the United Kingdom by Oxford University Press

British Library Cataloguing in Publication Data

Data available

ISBN 0 19 917445 8

10 9 8 7 6 5 4 3 2

Also available in packs
Communications Mixed Pack (one of each book) ISBN 0 19 917446 6
Communications Class Pack (six of each book) ISBN 0 19 917447 4

www.oup.com/uk/primary

Printed in China

Acknowledgements

The Publisher would like to thank the following for permission to reproduce photographs:
p 4 Mary Evans Picture Library (top right), Telegraph Colour Library (bottom left),
Bruce Coleman/J & P Wegner (bottom right); p 5 Oxford Scientific Films/M Hill (centre right),
Bruce Coleman/J & P Wenger (bottom left); p 7 TCL/K Lucas (top right), Mary Evans Picture
Library (centre left); p 8 Corbis UK; p 9 OSF/M Hill; p 10 Bruce Coleman/H Reinhard;
p 11 OSF/K Wothe; p 12 Bruce Coleman; p 13 Corbis UK; p 14 TCL/Planet Earth/J Lythgoe;
p 15 OSF/M Fogden; p 16 OSF/M Hamblin; p 17 Bruce Coleman (all); p 18 Corbis Uk (top),
OSF/M Plage (bottom); p 19 OSF/M Plage (top); p 20 Corbis UK (bottom); p 21 Magnum/
M Nichols (top); p 22 Corbis UK; p 23 OSF/F Schneidermeyer; p 24 Corbis UK (all); p 25 Mary
Evans Picture Library (top), Bruce Coleman/H Reinhard (bottom); p 27 Werner Forman Archive;
p 28 Kenna Bourke (top); p 29 Corbis UK (top left), OSF/W Paton (top right), OSF/M Hamblin
(bottom right), OSF/T Tilford (bottom left); p 30 Corbis UK.

Additional photography OUP ©

Front cover photograph by Telegraph Colour Library/G Shumway

Illustrated by Martin Aston, Stefan Chabluk, Michael Courtney and Roger Gorringe

Contents

Introduction   4

Communication between animals of the same species

Chapter 1   Communicating about food   6

Chapter 2   Talking about danger   9

Chapter 3   Keeping together   11

Chapter 4   Showing off   13

Communication between animals of different species

Chapter 5   Warning off the enemy   16

Chapter 6   Helping each other   18

Communication between humans and animals

Chapter 7   The great apes   20

Chapter 8   Bird brain?   23

Chapter 9   Man's best friends   24

Chapter 10   Companion animals   26

Glossary   31

Index   32

Introduction

The seventeenth-century French thinker and writer, Descartes, believed that animals were incapable of thoughts and feelings. He took the view that they didn't have language and were therefore just "machines".

If you compare a baby chimpanzee with a human baby, the differences are not very great. Both babies grab at objects, smile at friendly faces and scream when they're hurt, hungry or upset. Neither the chimpanzee nor the human baby has language, yet nobody would say that human babies were machines.

Three centuries after Descartes, with advances in science and animal research, we now know rather more about the way animals communicate.

▲ René Descartes thought that all animals were just "machines", as they didn't have language.

▼ Human babies and baby chimpanzees communicate in a similar way.

The one thing animals don't do is talk in the way that humans do. One of the reasons for this is that they don't have the same **vocal** (voice) equipment as we do. Human mouths, lips and tongues are well suited to forming words. The voice box and **epiglottis** (the flap that stops food from going down your windpipe) are very good at controlling the flow of air, which also helps you to speak.

Nevertheless, like humans, animals communicate in a variety of ways. You may look sad when something upsets you, and so does a dog. You may shout to warn a friend of danger, and so does a vervet monkey. You may attract your friends' attention by changing your appearance – by dressing up for a party or painting your face – and the peacock, using his magnificent tail feathers, does just the same.

See pages 9 & 14

Dogs that are angry ▶
or frightened bare
their teeth.

▼ Human vocal equipment

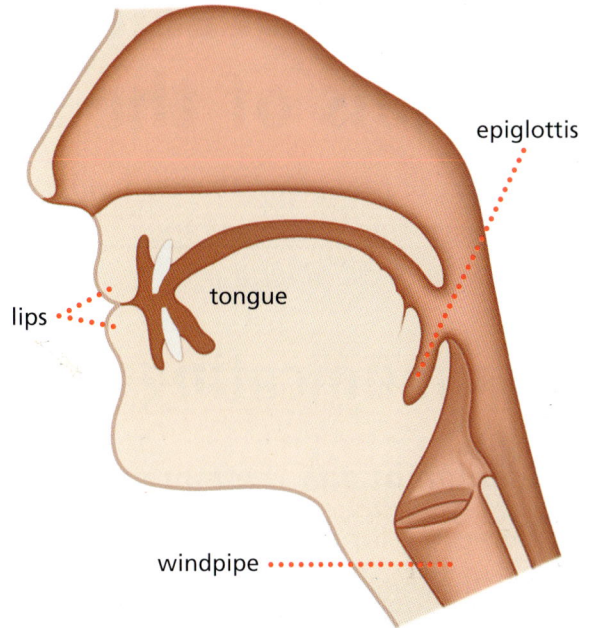

epiglottis

lips

tongue

windpipe

▲ Apes and monkeys are among the most intelligent species on earth.

This book looks at a number of **mammals**, birds and insects and explores the amazing ways they have of "talking". Birds, dolphins, whales and apes are the four groups of animals that have been studied the most. As you will see, their intelligence and ability to communicate with one another, and with humans, is remarkable.

5

Communication between animals of the same species

We can see or hear many animals communicating with others of their own kind. Communication between animals of the same species is called intraspecies communication.

Communicating about food

The dolphins and the moray eel

In the search for food, communication between animals of the same species is common.

Dolphins communicate with each other through a series of clicks and whistles.

Two captive dolphins were once seen displaying a clever way of co-operating with each other while hunting a moray eel. The eel was trying to hide in between two rocks in the dolphins' tank. First, one of the dolphins caught a scorpion fish, which has a poisonous spine. With the fish in its mouth, the dolphin touched the eel with the poisonous spine. The moray eel shot out of its hiding place, straight into the mouth of the second dolphin, which was waiting for it on the other side of the rocks.

See page 11

The dance of the honeybees

Many beekeepers and naturalists have noticed that bees return to the nest and tell other bees where the source of food is, but for centuries nobody knew how the bees passed on the information. Eventually, the mystery was solved by an Austrian zoologist, Karl von Frisch, in 1943. He discovered that bees like to dance when they find a source of **nectar**, **pollen** or water. The dance is almost a re-enactment of the journey that the bee has just made.

▲ Although we see honeycombs lying horizontally, the **combs** inside the nest are vertical.

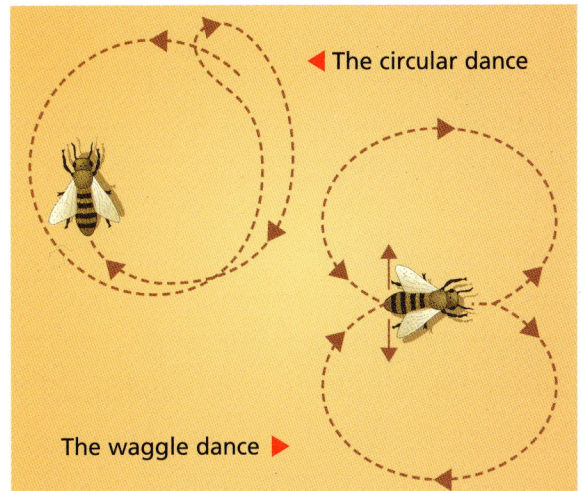

Karl von Frisch ▶ won the Nobel Prize for Medicine in 1973.

◀ The circular dance

The waggle dance ▶

The honeybee uses two types of dance – the "circular dance", which indicates that the flowers containing the nectar or pollen are a short distance away (50–80 metres), and the "waggle dance", for ood which is further away.

In the waggle dance, the returning bee crawls onto one of the **combs** near the entrance of the nest and performs a small figure of eight. This dance may go on for several minutes. As the bee dances, it waggles its **abdomen** vigorously, hence the name "waggle dance".

Using the sun as a compass, the bee then points out the exact location of the food. If the bee runs vertically up the side of the comb with a waggling movement, the flowers are to be found in the direction of the Sun. Flowers that are situated to the left or right of the Sun are indicated by a waggle to the left or right of the straight line.

Humphrey, the lost whale

Sometimes humans are able to use the animal's own sounds to "talk" to them. In October 1985, a young humpback whale, later nicknamed Humphrey, swam away from his **pod** (group) while **migrating** south from Alaska. He turned into San Francisco Bay and swam up the Sacramento River. When he had swum 50 kilometres up the river, rescuers set about guiding him back to the Pacific Ocean. They sailed behind him with "sound nets". A sound net is a group of small boats carrying people who make unpleasant noises by banging steel pipes together. The noise drove him away. Ahead of Humphrey, a boat broadcasting a recording of the humpback whale's feeding call chugged towards the open sea. Humphrey followed the familiar sounds and was safely returned to the ocean.

See page 12

ALASKA

CANADA

SACRAMENTO RIVER

U.S.A.

PACIFIC OCEAN

MEXICO

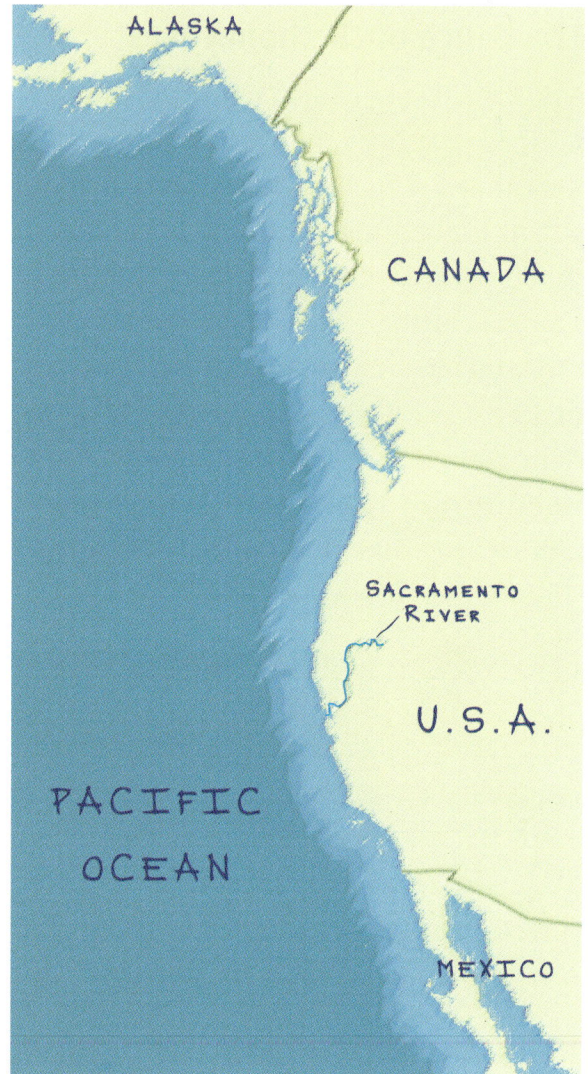

◀ This was not the only escapade Humphrey had. In 1990 he returned to San Francisco Bay and became stuck on a **mud flat**. This time rescuers pulled him off with the aid of a net and a coastguard boat.

Talking about danger

peacock

Asian deer

Most animals have **predators** that hunt and kill them. To protect themselves and each other, many animals make sounds that signal danger. Usually the alarm call is to warn animals of the same species that there is a predator nearby, but some animals that share the same habitat learn to recognize each other's alarm calls. The langur monkeys of Asia, for instance, react to the flight of the peacock and the alarm call of the deer.

langur monkey

▲ Vervet monkeys live in small groups and quickly learn to recognize each other's alarm calls.

The alarm call of the vervet monkey

Vervet monkeys, which are found in Africa, use different alarm calls for different predators. Vervets are preyed upon by lions, cheetahs, eagles and snakes. When a vervet hears the eagle alarm call, it hides in thick grass or bushes so that it cannot be seen from the air. On hearing the snake alarm call, vervets scramble to safety, high in a tree.

How Thumper got his name

Rabbits use their powerful back legs to thump loudly on the ground. This warns other rabbits of danger. Pet rabbits behave in the same way. Even if they are the only rabbit in a house, they thump to alert humans to danger. The danger may not be a real one: rabbits are easily alarmed by unusual sounds. An aeroplane flying overhead may lead a pet rabbit to thump.

(See page 28)

The tail-slapping beaver

Beavers are preyed upon by several animals including foxes, owls, hawks, and alligators. One sound that beavers are well known for making is the "tail slap". They bring their tails down flat against the water and make a loud slapping noise to warn other beavers that there is a **predator** about.

◀ Some people believe that the tail-slapping also acts as a signal to predators to keep away. The predator is frightened off by the loud noise.

Keeping together

The friendly dolphin

Dolphins do not have **vocal** cords, but they are able to make clicks and whistles which they use to communicate and navigate underwater. The clicking system is called **echolocation**. The clicks travel through the water, bounce off objects, and return as echoes to inform the dolphin of the exact location of the object.

WHISTLING DOLPHINS

New dolphin behaviour has recently been discovered. Dolphins greet their friends using individual whistles. Until now this sort of behaviour has only been found in birds and humans. Each dolphin has its own unique whistle and can mimic another dolphin's whistle after hearing it just once.

Nearly two thousand whistles from dolphin colonies off the Scottish coast have been recorded by scientists. The dolphins answer each other by mimicking each other's whistles. Interactions like these are thought to be a first step towards the evolution of real language.

Communication between dolphins is obviously quite sophisticated, but just what they are saying to each other no one really knows.

◄ Dolphins make the clicking sound using their **nasal** sacs. These are located behind the melon, which is the bump on their foreheads.

See page 6

The song of the humpback whale

The song of the male humpback whale is one of the most fascinating examples of long distance communication. It is not yet certain why these whales sing, but researchers believe it is either to attract a mate or to warn off rivals.

Whales are to be ▶ found in all the oceans of the world.

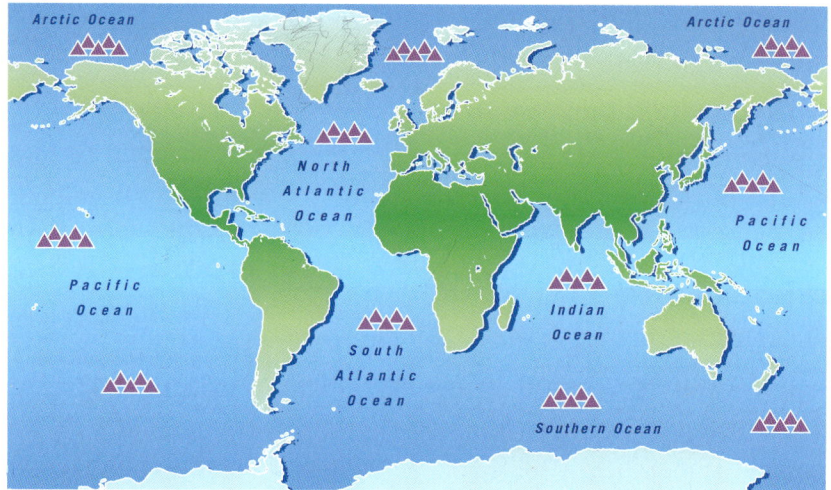

All the male whales living in a particular area sing exactly the same song. So, for example, all the whales in the North Atlantic sing one song, yet the whales of the Pacific sing another.

The song of the humpback whale is composed of a series of melodies and verses which are repeated over and over again. The song can be heard hundreds of kilometres away.

The whales sing continuously for between six and eighteen minutes on average. As the weeks go by, the song changes slightly, with the whales adding new noises and dropping others. The following year, a new song starts where the last year's song ended.

▲ People have described the whales' song as eerie, beautiful and haunting. Some of the notes that the whales sing are too low to be heard by humans.

See page 8

12

Showing off

▲ Frigate birds are also very good at flying. In some areas they are known as the "pirates of the sky".

The frigate bird

Just like humans, animals sometimes want to impress each other. Birds are probably the masters of this art. Usually they show off in order to attract a mate.

The male frigate bird is particularly good at showing off his beauty when a female frigate bird is around. To impress the female, the frigate bird tilts his head back and begins to **inflate** a pouch under his neck to reveal a splendid, bright red heart shape. This display can take up to 20 minutes. While the pouch is inflating, the bird **vibrates** his wings rapidly, and makes loud clicking and drumming sounds.

The peacock

The national bird of India, the peacock, is famous for his dazzling display of tail feathers. Again, the peacock does this in order to attract a female as a mate. The peacock performs a courtship display. He starts by offering the female a tantalizing bit of food. If the female accepts the food, the peacock starts to spread his magnificent tail feathers and makes long hissing sounds as he walks in circles round the female.

▲ Each of the peacock's tail feathers has an "eye". These are called the **ocelli**.

◀ The peahen is attracted by this magnificent sight.

The bower bird

Not all birds rely on their looks or voices to impress each other. Some use the things around them to show off. The bower bird is the "interior designer" of the bird world. To attract a mate, it builds a house and then decorates it. Using twigs, leaves and moss, the bird first constructs a **bower** – a kind of shelter. It then decorates the bower with as many colourful objects as it can find, from feathers and shells to pebbles and bottle caps. When the bower is finished, the bird waits for a female to inspect its handiwork.

◀ The bower is so important to the bird that males will often steal objects from each other to decorate them.

Communication between animals of different species

Some animals are able to communicate with animals of other kinds. Communication between animals of different species is called interspecies communication.

Warning off the enemy

The skylark

Bird song is one of the most effective kinds of communication. Birds can produce a much greater variety of sounds than humans can, thanks to their complex **vocal** equipment. Sound travels in all directions, and even through and round objects, which means that the song can be heard even if the bird cannot be seen. Birds sing to communicate with other birds, and also to warn off **predators**.

The skylark, which is preyed upon by other birds such as the sparrowhawk, the merlin and the peregrine, is particularly famous for its song. The ability to sing and fly at the same time sends a message to the predator that the lark is very fit and will be difficult to catch. Skylarks are so impressive that great poets like Shakespeare and Shelley wrote poems about them.

▲ The skylark soars almost vertically into the air until it reaches a great height, singing all the way.

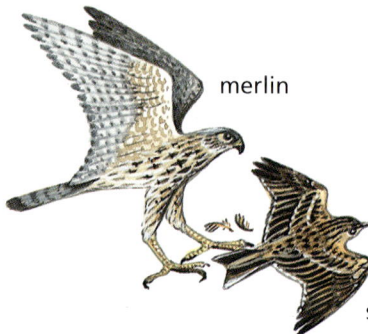

sparrowhawk

merlin

peregrine falcon

skylark

16

Porcupines and rattlesnakes

There are animals like porcupines and rattlesnakes which have clever ways of scaring off the enemy. They make terrible rattling sounds. The porcupine does this by shaking its quills (the long spikes on its body) which sends out a clear message to any would-be predator: stay away!

Mostly predators do stay away because the porcupine's quills can quite easily become detached and stick into the attacker's skin. They can inflict painful wounds. When threatened by a predator, the porcupine hides its snout safely between its front legs and spins round to show its spikey back to the enemy.

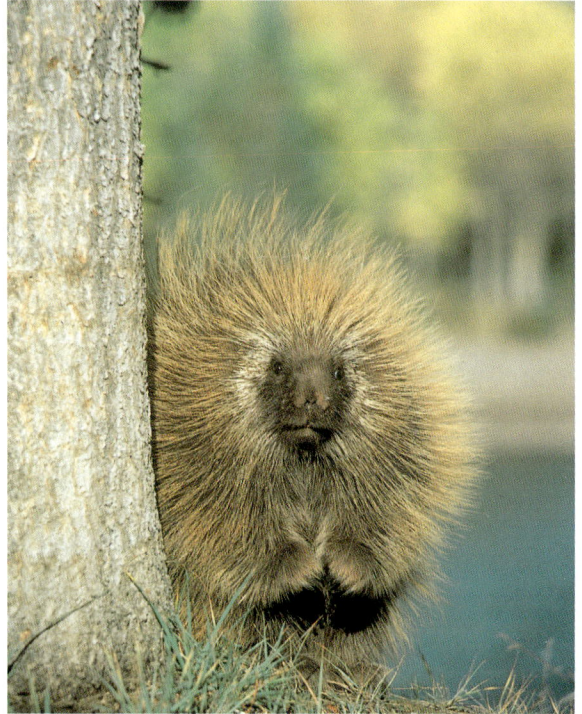

▲ Porcupines can have up to 30,000 quills on their bodies.

The rattlesnake has a ▶ rattle on the tip of its tail. When the snake feels threatened, it shakes the rattle to warn off the attacker.

Helping each other

Occasionally animals need to ask each other for a little help. Often these requests are connected with food.

The honeyguide and the honey badger

The African honeyguide is a cunning bird. It likes to feast on beeswax and bee **larvae**. Although it can easily find bees' nests, it cannot get into them. The honey badger loves honey but is not very good at finding bees' nests. These two creatures have forged a partnership in the quest for food.

▲ The honey badger's real name is a ratel. It is not a badger at all but looks quite like one.

▼ A honeyguide

The honeyguide, on finding a bees' nest, flutters its wings and calls noisily until a honey badger appears. It then waits until the honey badger has climbed the tree, pulled open the nest and eaten the honey. Only then does the honeyguide get its feast of wax and larvae.

The woodpecker finch and the cactus finch

Another clever bird is the woodpecker finch. This finch lives in the Galapagos islands and is one of the few members of the animal kingdom known to use a tool to trap its food. Woodpecker finches use a twig or a long spine from a cactus plant to spear a grub or force it out of its hiding place.

More remarkable still was the discovery that, when in captivity together, cactus finches learned this skill by watching woodpecker finches, and in turn started to use tools to capture insects.

The use of tools by animals is considered one of the main signs of intelligence. Humans communicate information to each other by demonstrating how to do things. Now we know some animals do it too.

▲ In captivity, the cactus finch learnt how to use a tool like this one. The woodpecker finch "teacher" helped the cactus finch "pupil" by passing a ready-made spine across for the cactus finch to use. You learn how to do things by watching and copying.

The carrion crow

Occasionally humans can be called upon to give a helping hand to animals. In Japan, crows have been seen placing walnuts on pedestrian crossings. They wait patiently for the traffic lights to turn red, hop across the road to place the walnuts in front of the cars, go back and wait for the cars to run over the nuts, then hop back to pick up the freshly-cracked goodies.

◀ A carrion crow on the road

Communication between humans and animals

For centuries, people have studied and recorded examples of animals communicating with humans.

The great apes

Chimpanzees

We share 99 per cent of our **genes** with chimpanzees, so it is not surprising that humans thought them the most likely candidates for conversation. Early attempts in the 1930s and 40s to make chimpanzees produce real speech failed, so researchers hit upon another method: sign language.

This is the ASL ▶ sign for "happy".

Several chimpanzees have been taught to "talk" thanks to the American Sign Language (ASL) system. In America there is a female chimpanzee called Washoe who apparently has a vocabulary of about 240 words.

Through chimpanzees like Washoe, we can develop a number of theories. Firstly, chimpanzees may have emotions. Some chimpanzees seem to notice when other chimpanzees or humans are hurt or upset and make the ASL signs for "sorry" and "hurt". Secondly, it is possible that they know the difference between good and bad. People have observed chimpanzees scolding each other for bad behaviour.

◀ Not everyone agrees that chimpanzees understand the signs they make. Some people think that they are simply imitating humans.

Amazingly, some people think that chimpanzees can invent new words. One chimpanzee signed "drink fruit" when shown a watermelon, another described a radish as "cry hurt food" because it tasted hot. This possibility is important to researchers because it suggests that the apes have a sense of **logic** and a desire to express themselves.

The bonobos

It has been said that trying to teach an animal to communicate is as silly as trying to teach a human to fly. Dr Savage-Rumbaugh would not agree. She has worked with two very special **pygmy** chimpanzees (bonobos) called Kanzi and Panbanisha.

These are the ▶ symbols on Kanzi's keypad for "go" and "blueberries".

▲ Kanzi points at pictures as he hears the words through his headphones.

Kanzi was the first ape to learn language in the same way that children learn it, by listening and observing, rather than being trained. To communicate with humans, he uses a keypad that triggers a **synthetic voice**. Kanzi was very quick to learn symbols for things he was interested in, like other bonobos' names, and the words for his favourite foods.

CHIMP ASKS FOR ICED COFFEE!

from our Science correspondent

A bonobo chimpanzee by the name of Panbanisha knows 3000 words and talks through a computer that produces a synthetic voice as she presses symbols on a keyboard. She is now quite a chatterbox; making sentences like "Please can I have an iced coffee?" The bonobos have been taught to use a specially designed keypad with about 400 keys, each bearing a symbol. Some keys have simple meanings such as "apple" and "coffee"; others represent more difficult ideas such as "give me", "good" or "help".

Panbanisha's mother, Matata, cannot use the keyboard, so she gets Panbanisha to communicate for her, by saying things like: "Matata wants a banana."

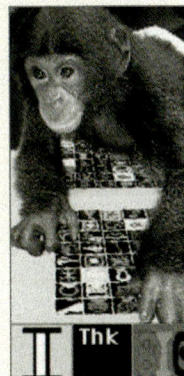

The bonobos teach their skills to their offspring.

Gorillas

Chimpanzees are not the only apes to have these communication skills. At Project Koko, a gorilla called Koko has not only mastered ASL, but uses it to make jokes.

She is a stubborn gorilla, according to her trainer, Dr Francine Patterson. One day, Koko was being trained to learn the names of the parts of the body. She quickly became bored and signed: "Think eye-ear-eye-nose boring!"

Koko particularly dislikes one of the researchers at Project Koko. His name is Ron. When Patterson asked the simple question "Who Ron?", Koko quickly signed "stupid devil".

Koko enjoys a chat with Dr Patterson ▶

Bird brain?

Alex, the African grey parrot

Many parrots and other birds **mimic** human speech, simply repeating the words they hear. However, there is now evidence to suggest that some parrots can decide what to say. Alex is an African grey parrot who has learnt to do some remarkable things.

According to his trainer, Dr Pepperberg, Alex is capable of doing many of the things a young child can do. He can even tell her what he'd like to eat!

PRETTY POLLY?
No, clever Alex!

Alex has taken animal intelligence one step further. Talking is a skill we are used to seeing in parrots, but unlike many of his feathered friends, Alex means what he says. Dr Irene Pepperberg, Professor of Biology at the University of Arizona, has been training Alex since 1977.

Alex doesn't just talk. He can also identify fifty different objects, count to six, understand words such as bigger, smaller, same and different, and he can distinguish seven colours and five shapes. If you ask him what colour corn is, for example, he'll answer "yellow".

"Emotionally, parrots behave like spoilt two-year-olds," says Dr Pepperberg. "But intellectually he's up there with chimps and dolphins. He's doing the same tasks. It's remarkable."

◄ Alex, who says "Bye. You be good. I'm gonna go eat dinner. I'll see you tomorrow." to Dr Pepperberg every night as she leaves the laboratory.

Man's best friends

The dolphin – human connection

For thousands of years, people have had a soft spot for dolphins. The Ancient Greeks believed that a dolphin near a ship was a sign of good luck. Around AD 75 the writer, Plutarch, told the story of Korianos, who pleaded with fishermen to save the life of a dolphin caught in a fishing net. The dolphin was released unharmed. Later, Korianos was shipwrecked and his own life was saved by a dolphin.

It would seem that we have never lost our love of dolphins. These days many sick people swim with dolphins in order to get better. People with cancer, children who have difficulty expressing themselves, and people who have previously been very unhappy have all reported an improvement in health after being in contact with a dolphin.

▲ Dolphins seem to like us, too. In the Red Sea on the Sinai peninsula, at a place called Nuweiba, lives a dolphin named Oline. She is frequently to be seen in the shallow waters swimming with people, just for fun.

◄ As early as 1600 BC, the dolphin featured in art. This is a fresco painted on the queen's bathroom wall at the palace of Knossos in Crete.

Greyfriars Bobby

Dogs are often described as man's best friend. We are more used to communicating with them than any other animal. Dogs seem to regard humans as part of their "pack".

Dogs perform amazing tasks for us, from St Bernard dogs who show rescuers where to find injured people in the mountains, to sniffer dogs who lead us to people buried under the rubble in an earthquake.

Many blind people and deaf people rely on guide dogs to help them cope with daily life.

One of the most touching stories was heard in 1858, in Edinburgh. A Skye terrier by the name of Bobby had a master called John Grey, to whom he was devoted. When John Grey died, Bobby followed his master's coffin as it was carried to Greyfriars churchyard. After the burial, Bobby refused to leave the graveside and remained there in a shelter specially made for him until his own death nearly 15 years later.

The relationship John Grey had formed with Bobby was as strong as many that exist between humans. Some people would say that dogs are not capable of love, and yet Bobby displayed an affection for his master that many would be envious of.

◀ When Bobby died in 1873, a memorial was built to mark the little dog's loyalty to his master.

Seals to the rescue

Sometimes communication between humans and animals happens in ways we do not yet understand.

In England in 1999, a woman got into difficulty while swimming in the sea. To the amazement of the coastguard rescuers who arrived by boat to save her, she was discovered alive. She had been prevented from drowning by six seals who surrounded her and kept her afloat.

▲ A grey seal

Companion animals

Here are some things you can do to observe animal communication for yourself.

Watch your dog

Study as many different kinds of dog as possible. See how their hackles (the hairs on the backs of their necks) rise when they feel threatened by other dogs. When two dogs meet, watch carefully to see what happens. In order to avoid a fight, dogs need to determine which of the two of them is the superior dog. One of them does this by rolling over on the ground, or lying very flat, to show that they are the weaker dog.

Watch how dogs growl and bark when they feel angry and want to keep another animal or person away. Make a note of what they do with their teeth.

Try to notice the different sounds dogs make. For instance, they whimper when they are upset or unwell. They

▲ The dog on the left is the "top dog".

make short, yapping sounds when they are excited. Listen to the way they bark when they want your attention. Compare this with their behaviour when they are happy.

26

The graceful cat

Humans have loved cats since the time of the Ancient Egyptians. Cats were so highly thought of by the Egyptians that they were even buried in pyramids with their owners.

▲ A frightened or angry cat is easy to spot.

Pet cats have several ways of communicating, both with each other and with us. Make a note of all the different ways a cat communicates. Look at what it does with its tail when it is angry, when it is about to pounce, and when it is relaxed. Watch the way it sits and lies.

A cat's ears are a good indicator of how it feels. They will prick forward when the cat is alert but lie almost flat against its head when it feels either aggressive or frightened.

How does a cat behave towards a human when it wants food? Watch the way it moves and the sounds it makes.

◄ A mummified cat – the Ancient Egyptians believed that cats would accompany their owners into the next world.

How to listen to your rabbit

Although rabbits don't make very many noises, they do make some. A rabbit that is annoyed, or about to attack, makes a growling noise as it pounces.

Listen very, very carefully to a rabbit that is relaxed. If you are lucky, you will hear a tooth-grinding noise, which indicates that the rabbit is happy and contented.

A happy rabbit will often perform a kind of mad dance which involves running very fast and doing a back-flip in mid air. This lets you, and other rabbits, know that it is happy.

Watch and see if you can spot a rabbit throwing itself onto one side. It suddenly flops. This may look quite alarming but all it means is that the rabbit is relaxed and contented.

Write down all the things you see a rabbit do with its ears. Rabbits use their ears to show exactly how they feel:

See page 10

happy, frightened, or aggressive. See if you can work out what each position means.

Believe it or not, rabbits sulk. They turn their backs on people and other rabbits they are angry with. Watch carefully! Your rabbit may be trying to tell you something.

On the other hand, if a rabbit licks you, it's not just that it thinks you taste nice, it's his or her way of saying "I love you".

◀ Animals that are at ease often groom themselves.

Garden birds

Garden birds are ideal to watch and listen to. A good way to start is by putting a bird feeder with safe seeds and nuts in the garden, or at school, to attract the birds. Keep a notebook with you to list the forms of communication you see.

The robin has a red ▶ chest for a very good reason. It says "danger, keep away." Robins are very **territorial** birds so it is likely that you will only see one at a time.

Blackbirds have a very distinctive alarm call. See if you can identify it. Usually they fly away as they make the sound. Watch to see what they do with their tail feathers.

◀ A male blackbird

Starlings are extremely good **mimics**. They sometimes imitate a telephone ringing. They can also be quite noisy and aggressive towards other birds, particularly when there is food around. Watch how they behave at a bird table, for example.

▲ Starlings investigating a rubbish bin

If you are lucky enough to see collared doves, look out for the mating dance they do to attract one another.

▲ Collared doves

Between March and August you can see young sparrows urging their parents to feed them. Notice how they attract their parents using their wings.

Conclusion

Almost any animal, bird or insect you care to mention has its own special way of communicating. Just by looking around you, you can observe this for yourself.

Look at ants, for instance. Ants communicate with each other partly by leaving chemical trails behind them. No doubt you have noticed the way ants walk behind one another in a straight line. They are literally following their noses.

"Are you sure we're going the right way?"

From the tiny ant to the majestic elephant, communication is taking place. Recent studies on the trumpeting calls of wild elephants have shown that there is truth in the old saying "An elephant never forgets." Female elephants can recognize up to a hundred of their friends, and remember friends and family even after a gap of several years.

One night, when you are lying in bed and all appears to be quiet, listen carefully and remember that whether it's high up in the sky with the lark, or deep under the ocean with the whales, it's a noisy old world out there!

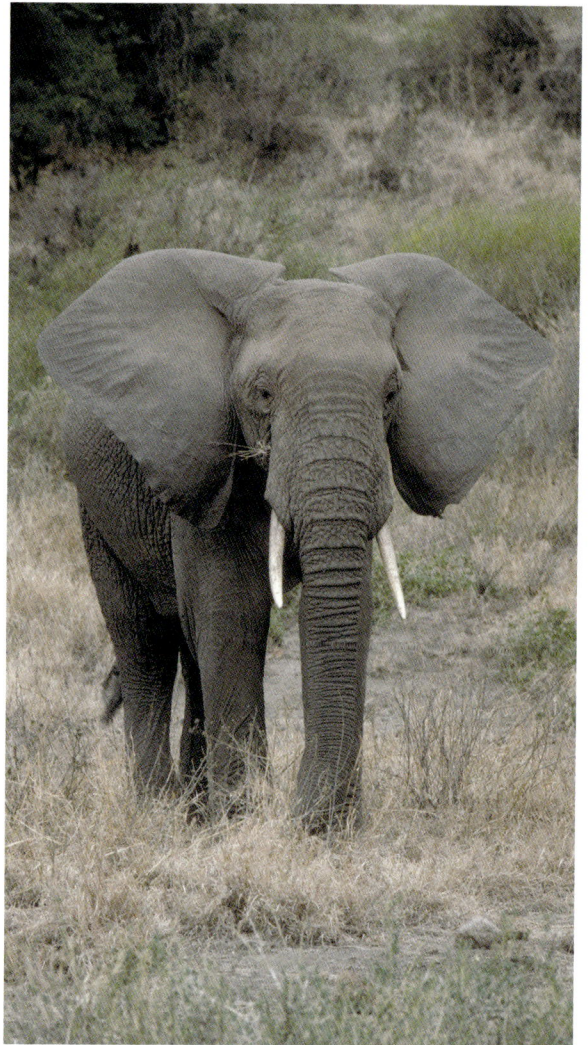

▲ Each elephant has its own unique call. They keep in touch with each other through low-pitched rumbles which can be heard several kilometres away.

Glossary

abdomen 1) stomach, 2) the back part of an insect's body

bower a leafy shelter

comb a structure made by bees for storing honey

echolocation a way of finding objects using supersonic vibrations

epiglottis a small flap over the entrance to the windpipe

gene a unit of DNA which passes on characteristics such as eye colour from parents to children

inflate blow up

larva a very young insect which looks very different from the adult, e.g. a caterpillar

logic the method we use to think and make sensible decisions

mammal the class of animals that feeds its young, e.g. humans, dogs, dolphins

migration a change from one country to another

mimic to copy or imitate

mud flat a muddy stretch of land

nasal to do with the nose

nectar the honey found in plants

ocelli the "eyes" on a peacock's tail feathers

pod a group of whales

pollen a powder found in flowers

predator an animal that kills and eats another animal

pygmy a very small person, animal or thing

synthetic voice a voice made by a computer to sound like a human voice

territorial wanting to defend a stretch of land

vibrate move continuously and rapidly to and fro

vocal to do with the voice

Index

African grey parrot 23
Ancient Egyptians 27
ant 30

beaver 10
bee 7
blackbird 29
bonobo 21
bower bird 15

cactus finch 19
cat 27
chimpanzee 20
collared dove 29
crow 19

Descartes 4
dog 25, 26
dolphin 6, 11, 24

echolocation 11
elephant 30

frigate bird 13

gorilla 22
Greyfriars Bobby 25

honey badger 18

honeyguide 18
humpback whale 8, 12

Knossos 24

langur monkey 9

Patterson, Dr 22
peacock 5, 14
Pepperberg, Dr 23
porcupine 17

rabbit 10, 28
rattlesnake 17
robin 29

Savage-Rumbaugh, Dr 21
skylark 16
sparrow 29
St Bernard 25
starling 29

vervet monkey 9
von Frisch, Karl 7

waggle dance 7
whale song 8, 12
woodpecker finch 19